Ok Boomer THE COLORING BOOK
A coloring book filled with calming patterns for the millennial in all of us!
Pull yourself up by your bootstraps, Snowflake.
I0840491

Thank you for purchasing one of my coloring books!
I truly hope you enjoy it.

As we all know, reviews are the lifeblood of book sales so, if possible, please leave an Amazon review if you especially loved the coloring book.

I also love hearing from customers so feel free to email me at ElaineKayDesigns@gmail.com for any reason. This includes placing bulk orders or if you want to get on my mailing list so that you can be informed of future book releases and special deals.

OK
BOOMER

THIS IS WHAT A REAL
MAN LOOKS LIKE!

BACK IN THE
80'S WE
HAD 5
CHANNELS...
AND WERE
HAPPY!

BACK IN MY DAY WE
KNEW STYLE!

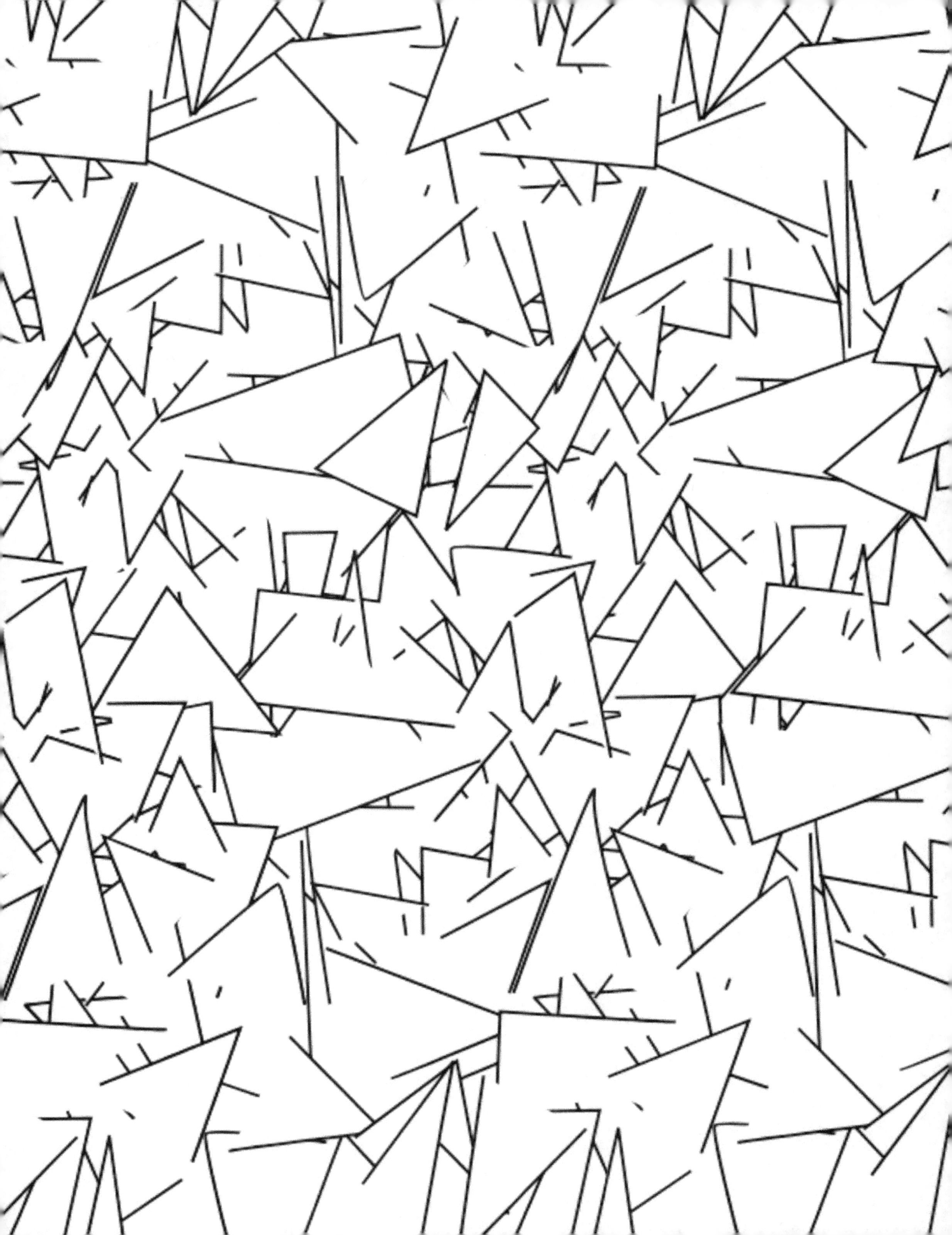

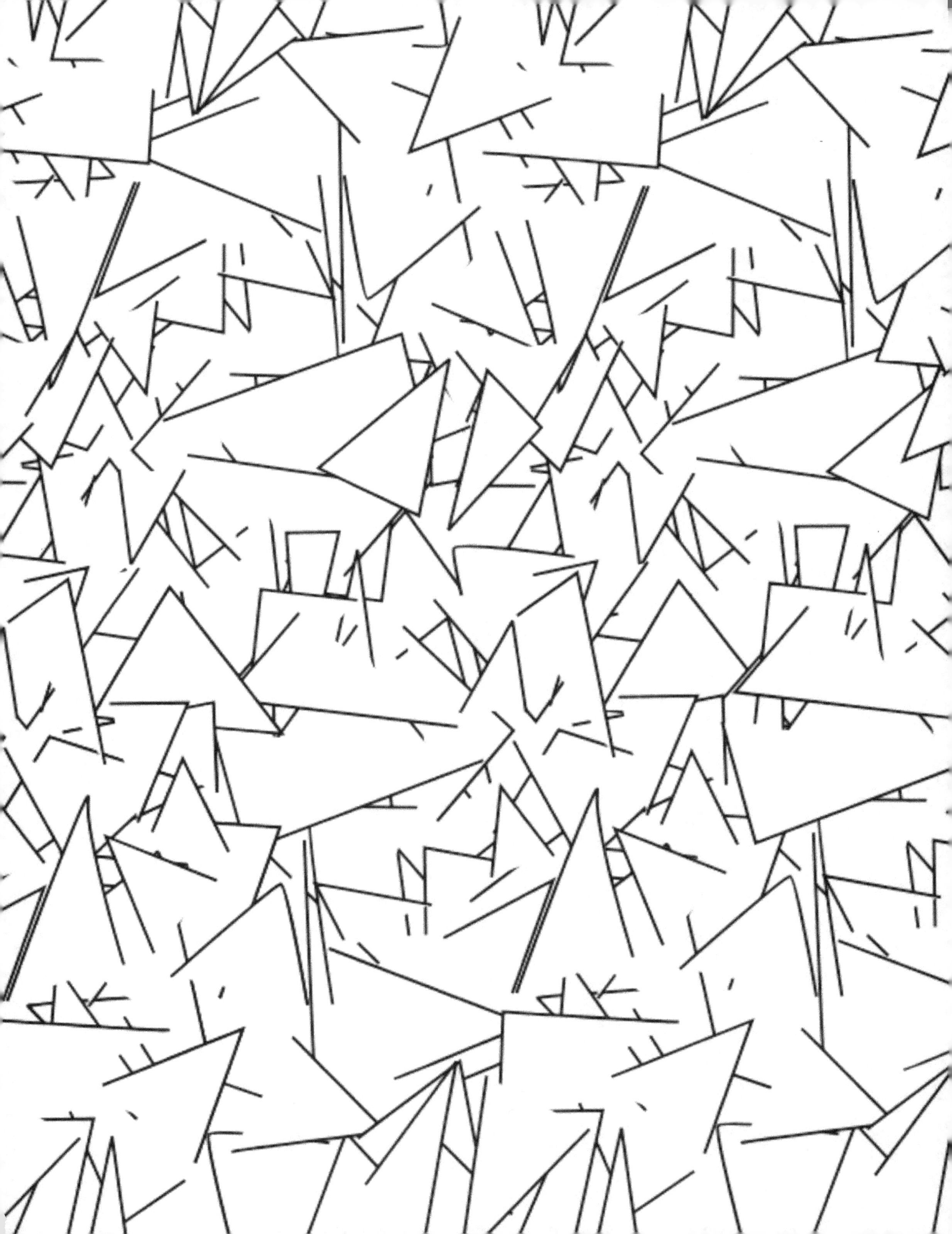

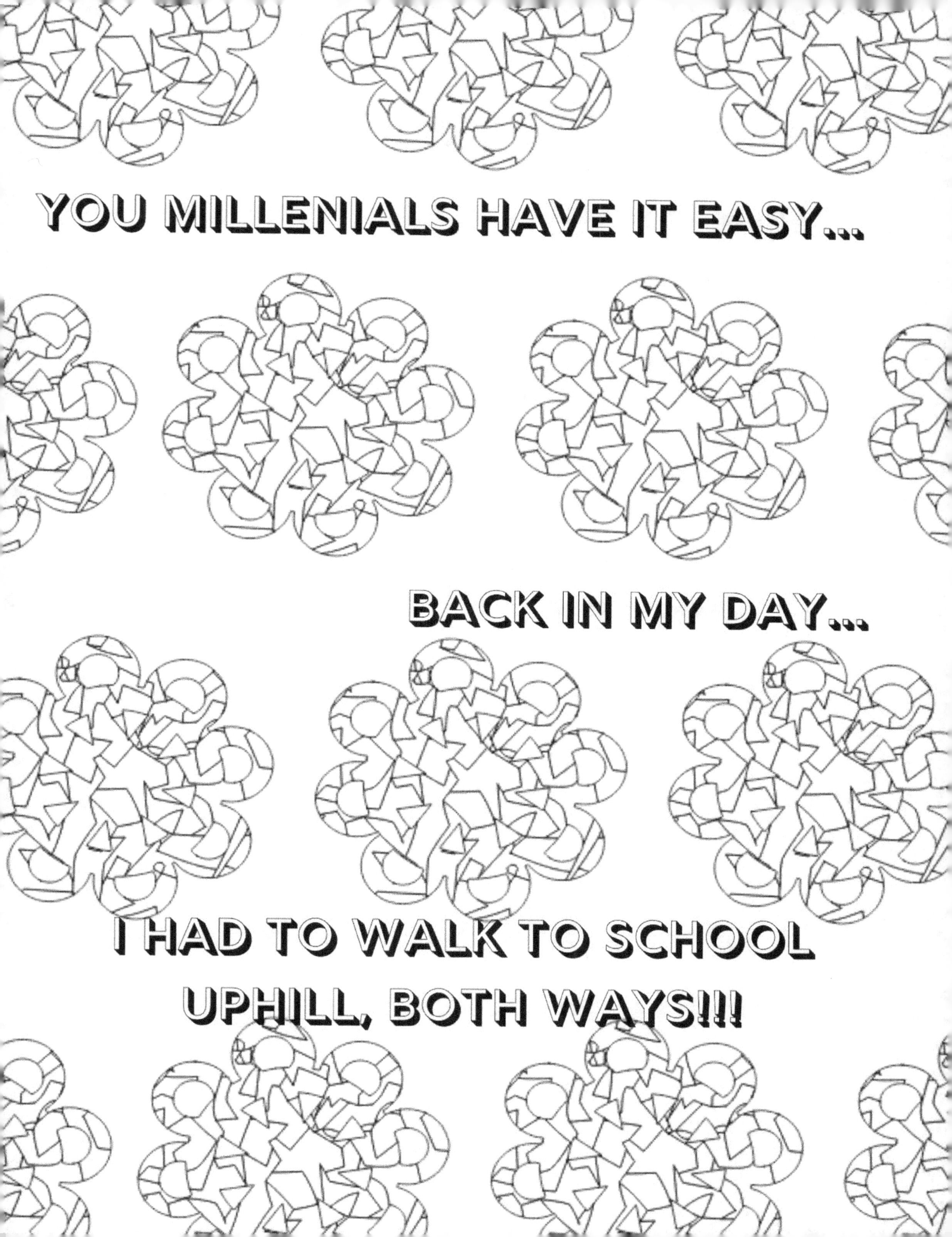

YOU MILLENIALS HAVE IT EASY...
BACK IN MY DAY...
I HAD TO WALK TO SCHOOL
UPHILL, BOTH WAYS!!!

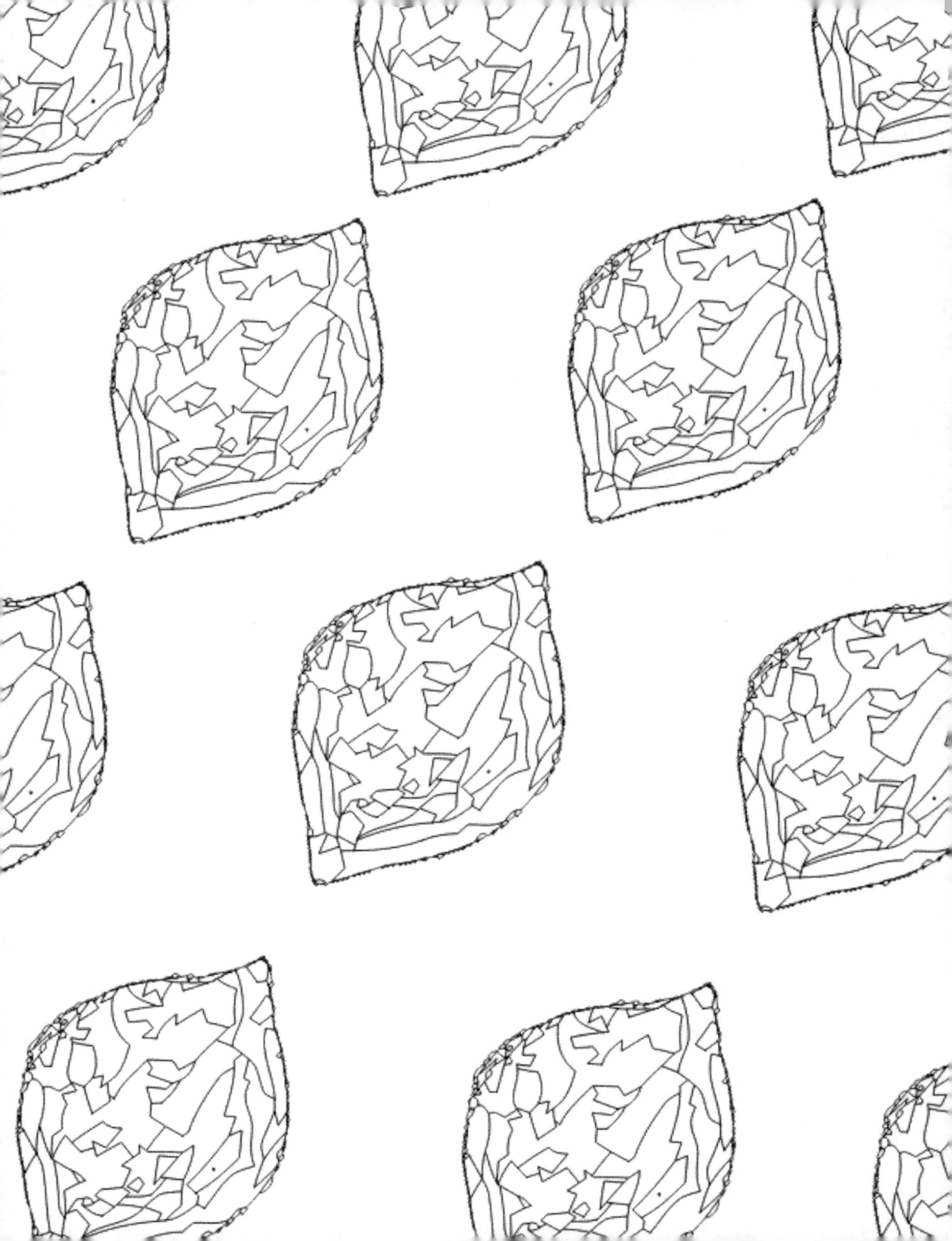

I BOUGHT A HOUSE AT 18!